STABILITY AND CHANGE IN LITERACY LEARNING/ *Holdaway*

By the same author:

*THE FOUNDATIONS OF LITERACY*
*INDEPENDENCE IN READING*

# Stability and Change in Literacy Learning

## Don Holdaway

HEINEMANN EDUCATIONAL BOOKS
Portsmouth, New Hampshire
and
THE ALTHOUSE PRESS
THE UNIVERSITY OF WESTERN ONTARIO
London, Ontario, Canada

Reprinted 1985, 1986, 1988

**Editor:** G. Milburn
**Editorial Assistant:** B. Nelson
**Cover Design:** Bothwell Graphics


Published in the U.S.A. by Heinemann Educational Books, Inc., 70 Court Street, Portsmouth, New Hampshire, 03801

ISBN 0-435-08209-4

**Library of Congress Cataloging in Publication Data**
Holdaway, Don.
   Stability and change in literacy learning.

   Bibliography: p.
   1. Developmental reading.  2. Learning.  3. Literacy.
I. Title.
LB1050.53.H64 1983  1983  428.4  83-22636
ISBN 0-435-08209-4




Published in Canada by The Althouse Press, Faculty of Education, The University of Western Ontario, 1137 Western Road, London, Ontario, Canada.

ISBN 0-920354-09-2

**Canadian Cataloguing in Publication Data**
Holdaway, Don.
   Stability and change in literacy learning.

   Bibliography: p.
ISBN 0-920354-09-2

1. Reading (Primary).  2. Literacy.  I. University of Western Ontario. Faculty of Education.  II. Title.

LB1525.H64  1983  372.4'1  C83-099199-9




Printed and bound in Canada by The Aylmer Express Limited, 17-23 King Street, Aylmer, Ontario, Canada N5H 1Z9

# CONTENTS

# PREFACE

I am deeply grateful for the real friendships and confront-
ations with nature which have informed my schoolboy
"knowledge" of Canada during my fifteen month stay. I am
grateful too for the professional richness of the experience
and especially for the academic sanctuary I found in The
University of Western Ontario. Although not addressed
specifically to the Canadian experience, this small book
makes an inadequate gesture of thanks and goodwill.

In days gone by the Antipodes were imagined to be in-
habited by strange and fabulous creatures, and I must
sometimes have appeared to my Canadian hosts as just such a
one. Although I would not insult my fellow islanders by
pretending to be typical of my race, the New Zealander carries something of the wave-tumbled isolation of his in-
heritance into the electronic age — a sort of haunted jet-lag, a
startled stare of apprehension at a world already made, and
an anachronistic certainty of having arrived late. At the same
time, the New Zealander cherishes a traditional impatience
for world-awareness which is driven by a sense of inferiority
and is sustained at home by a tradition of compulsive reading
and a remarkably comprehensive press. When vicarious
knowledge from reading suddenly encounters the real thing
head on there are likely to be temporary dissonances on both
sides, but the lasting impact is one of enrichment and fraternity.

The profession of teaching is rapidly becoming an *international* fraternity. Not that we are anywhere near to achieving a universal consensus on critical issues: it is the bewildering confusion of current controversy which provides the special context for this brief, precautionary contribution. I believe that international research and development in the field of literacy learning offers a salutary perspective on current priorities.

Originally, I undertook a comprehensive discussion of current issues in terms of this international perspective but soon found myself overwhelmed by the sheer size and complexity of the task. I decided, instead, to sketch an introductory overview which yet retained immediate classroom utility. The larger task will undoubtedly plague me in the months and years ahead, and will probably defeat me. However, it is my hope that this modest tract will encourage a studious, creative, and joyful exploration of developmental strategies in supporting early literacy.

*Don Holdaway*

# CHAPTER 1

# Research and Common Sense in Literacy Development

The current turmoil of our everyday lives is sufficient to remind us of all the clichés about modern change. How does the language teacher of the eighties maintain a sense of direction as the kaleidoscope trembles? Communications and computer technology, a massive externalization of human intelligence, mirrors and magnifies the processes of literacy before we have come properly to understand those processes in ourselves. People like McLuhan, who emphasized the power of the medium *as* message, do not strengthen our confidence as language teachers. *Is* literacy destined to decline? Concerned as we are with two of the most complex and least understood of human behaviors, literacy and learning, this question further unnerves us.

In fact, however, predictions concerning a decline in the use of literacy have been made false by the unprecedented explosion of print in the world of the seventies and eighties, from advertising through every sector of life to computer programming. Even in supporting the great superstructure of TV, print dominates modern action. Print has entered into a new alliance with modern media and rendered itself indispensible in the most surprising contexts. We must now, for instance, learn to read and write new computer languages in order to control a precocious present which was so recently a child of the future.

Power resides more than ever in the ability to write. Reading, on the other hand, is essential to participation. How difficult that is today, even in one's own specialty! Where do we look for the stability which will sustain us through the print shock of the future?

Modern linguistic research — more scientific, descriptive, and ethnographic as it has become — returns us unexpectedly to some very basic values both human and humane. In simple words, the most important, attested conditions for efficient language learning are faith, hope, and an informed charity. Look at our babies. In them the very conditions which have sustained our human continuity and historicity in language embody an unshakeably stable efficiency of learning strategies. Natural language learning is as secure, yet at the same time as *complex*, as anything in the confusing world around us.

The complexity, of course, lies in the marvel of the young human brain (Smith, 1975). That is why "faith" is such an important element in language teaching — we *trust* our babbling babies. The first mistake which we must expose is that the great complexity embodied in linguistic learning cannot exist in the sophisticated technology or "method" of the teacher: it exists only in the mind of the learner. Without knowing how to get the full cooperation of that complex young mind, our instructional technology is futile — no more than "sounding brass or a tinkling cymbal." (There's *somebody* who knew about instructional priorities!)

Our most sophisticated linguistic studies have revealed our need for a foundation built on common sense while at the same time pointing with remarkable specificity to the need for radical changes in pedagogical procedures. From our peculiar vantage point in time the insights ratified by developmental and psycholinguistic research fall roughly into three categories: the simple and obvious, which the growing complexity and *hubris* of our profession has by-passed or obscured; the suggestive and arguable, which invite deeper study and clarification; and the shockingly unexpected, to which our assumptions about schooling have blinded us. These three categories provide a rational basis for professional activity characterized by stability in the obvious, research in the arguable, and urgent change in the unexpected.

By way of clarification, let me take a few examples in each of these categories, bearing in mind that, at this stage, they have been isolated from a wider theoretical context:

*The simple and obvious* (but in practice neglected or contradicted). There is an extremely high correlation between the quantity of material transacted in a beginning reading program and success or failure in later reading (e.g., Clay, 1967, pp. 13-17; and compare Guthrie, 1981). In school, slower progress children spend many weeks "on" a few pages of print — what I call "criminal print starvation." We urgently need a *massive* increase in quantity of print transacted in learning to read and write. Very effective means of doing so abound, e.g., read-along techniques (Chomsky, 1976), supported reading (Hoskisson, 1975), individualized reading (Veatch, 1968), the "favorite book syndrome" (Holdaway, 1979) and shared reading (Barrett, 1982).

Another extremely high correlation has been found to exist between knowledge of *writing* on entry to school and the ability to *read* at 8 years (e.g., Robinson, 1973; and compare Mason, 1980).

Instruction has persistently separated reading from writing in a way which would be insufferable in learning to listen and talk. The two modes form an integral nexus of learning around common processes, and this, too, may readily be reflected in teaching. There are no logical or practical excuses for the dismemberment of literacy — only instructional precedents. The current upsurge in writing research is welcome and overdue, but because of the exigencies of specialization, such research itself may also continue to lack proper articulation with reading.

The teacher of reading is a significantly more important variable than the methodology (commonly reported in the mountainous aridity of methodological research). The teacher must be revalidated as the executive agent in making professional decisions. That role has been increasingly usurped by narrowly methodological "experts", by hierarchically imposed prescriptive syllabuses, by media-agitated parents, and most powerfully by educational publishers with their "teacher-proof" packages.[1]

*The suggestive and arguable* (too often neglected by research). The automaticity upon which all mature language functioning rests may *not* be most rapidly mastered through initial learning which demands deliberate, analytical control or application of rule (Gough, 1976; Holdaway, 1979, pp. 85-86, 171-180; Terry, 1976). The experience of babies in mastering phoneme discrimination in oral language seems to support this contention but we don't yet know enough about the matter, especially for reading and writing. However, it is of the first importance and should have some priority in research.[2]

From a psycholinguistic point of view, we would like to speculate that mature reading takes place without auditory mediation and that the important meaning system of intonation in speech plays an insignificant part in reading and writing (e.g., Smith, 1978). There is much evidence that the lively recreation of intonation patterns characterizes successful early reading, but we are uncertain about its function either in learning to read or in mature comprehension. The area is notoriously difficult to study and we may have to wait many years before there are any definitive answers to the important questions (Lefevre, 1964).

Facility in the use of imaginative, vicarious and metaphorical modes of comprehension appears to be an important characteristic of successful readers and writers (e.g., Britton, 1970). How are these operations learned and can they be taught effectively? Discourse analysis and schema theory are rapidly extending our understanding of comprehension processes long neglected, but we remain remarkably ignorant about the non-referential functions of meaning which provide the deepest rewards of literacy. Because such matters are not conducive to favored research models, we are likely to remain ignorant about many central issues of our discipline. (See also Gamble and McFetridge, 1981.)

*The surprising or shocking* (areas for urgent reform). There is a high correlation between successful self-correction or self-regulation in the early stages of learning and later success or failure in reading (Clay, 1980). Traditional practice assumes that independence is a stage to be reached after learning to read rather than an integral process within early learning. Most traditional procedures in the teaching of both reading and writing actively discourage self-regulation and render the learner dependent on external correction. There is an urgent need for radical change in the teaching and reinforcement of self-direction from the earliest stages of literacy learning.

A majority of children who become optimal progress readers and writers enjoy a lengthy early stage of approximation in reading their favorite books and in the exploration of writing (e.g., Teale, 1981; Temple, Nathan and Burris, 1982).

Approximation, which is universally accepted and delighted in during early developmental learning such as the learning of speech, has not been tolerated traditionally in school instruction. There is urgent need for radical changes in attitude towards approximation and correction in early language learning. We need to redefine what we mean by "error" in reading and writing. *Every* reputable method of teaching reading and writing has displayed "assumptional blindness" in this area.

The criteria of "Instructional Level" (95% accuracy, 75% comprehension) applies to beginning readers, i.e., optimal learning occurs through processing print at this high level of success from the beginnings of formal instruction (Clay, 1980). Many assumptions about the "basics" of reading are shattered by this finding. ("How can a child read accurately without first learning all the words?" or "Surely, children have to know their phonics before they can read successfully!")

Successful children, those who are allowed the opportunity, simply function like human beings, i.e., in sensible and complex ways. They can speak the language, they know its syntax, they expect language to fit together sensibly, their brains are keen in following predictable structures, they draw sound conclusions from good illustrations, they know all sorts of bits and pieces about written language which are useless in isolation but very powerful when they hang together with all these other clues, so they *read*. Of course, if the "book" happens to be an example of semi-language which has been denatured in the interests of controlling vocabulary or phonic regularity, they may go to pieces, literally, and verify our false assumptions. Some early readers will succeed at this high level because someone has fouled things up by reading them the story one or more times before. Memorableness and familiarity aid them mightily — but that, of course, is cheating.

The sarcasm may be unkind but it is intended to underline the peculiar deviousness of assumptive thinking as it leads us a dance around unexamined presuppositions which attract and fascinate like bright light to a moth. That's what is happening when people preface their appeals by *"surely* this or that." Our escape from false assumptions depends on equalizing the light and seeing parts of reality within an illuminated whole. This is one reason why developmental, longitudinal and ethnographic research are so vital to our complex discipline.

## STABILITY AND COHERENCE

Not only should research be cleanly descriptive of what actually happens under real world circumstances but it should also cohere with a strong body of related insights before we imagine that we know what it means or vote for reform. Theory changes the content of fact. For instance, if we look upon language as a coded transaction of *meanings* rather than as an inventory of vocabulary strung together according to grammatical rules, the "fact" that a child fails in reading a story in a controlled primer reader becomes a different piece of information. Indeed, the very words "fails", "reading" and "story" in the last sentence mean quite different things from the point of view of the two theories. If we enrich our transactional theory further and regard reading and writing as a continuous developmental process similar to the mastery of speech, we have some very precise questions we want to ask about our child who cannot "read" the primer. Theory determines fact as much as fact determines theory. Hence, the interconnections and consistencies among our insights partly define them.

The examples cited above as obvious, arguable or shocking begin to cohere as their relationships become apparent. The simple sanity of seeing reading and writing as a unity akin to listening and speaking, learned by copious use in genuine transactions influenced by the human rather than the technological skill of the teacher, provides the stable foundation of a theory drilled in the bedrock of human experience. The *surprising* "facts" become more intelligible, but no less urgently shocking, as we relate them to a growing architecture: self-determination, persistently refining approximation, and a choice of task within the daily compass of success deeply characterize all the most efficient forms of learning. The growing coherence also favors a tentative interpretation of our puzzling and arguable questions, suggesting possible models for clarifying research and warning against taking up doctrinaire positions on these matters.

Working out apparent contradictions rigorously may also strengthen the structure. For instance, it would seem that the acceptance of early approximation in reading and spelling is in conflict with the notion of optimum learning at "instructional level" in the formal teaching of reading. The important words are "early" and "formal". If we regard literacy as a developmental task, there will be no "pre-reading" or "readiness" stage: the first experiences with print and written dialect in story or sign, in song or rhyme, will be regarded as the beginnings of literacy. What we call "beginning reading" or "formal instruction" will belong to a later stage of development. Every child should have a lengthy period of gradually refining approximation in reading and writing before any of the techniques which we associate with formal instruction begin. The important insight is that if the teacher *requires* reading he or she has selected, learning is likely to be optimal when the pupil can handle *that* material at a high level of accuracy and comprehension. When children select their own reading *for performance purposes* they, too, will select material which they can handle with satisfying success.

Further coherence in our insights may be provided by

interconnections between related social disciplines. Trends with remarkable similarity are arising from research and practice in all the "helping" or social service professions. In different disciplines, self-determination and self-respect are being identified as the appropriate primary goal for clients, and great energy is being expended in compensating for the "asylum effects" of service institutions such as hospitals, prisons and even the armed forces. Schools, too, generate "asylum effects," many of them detrimental to literacy learning. The "helping professions," such as teaching, all take the risk of making their clients dependent. In contrast, really skillful professionals make themselves redundant to their clients as quickly as possible.

# CHAPTER 2

# The Environments of Literacy Learning

The directions being defined by current movements in our profession are clearly pointing towards more natural and developmental ways of meeting our objectives. Unquestionably the most efficient learning environments we know are those centred on the conditions of the healthy home, and recent research has been reminding us of that fact with an almost cruel clarity. This is not to say that as skilled professionals we cannot, or should not, exceed the efficiency of natural developmental learning but rather that to do so this is the path we must most urgently pursue.

I make no apology for raising a number of broader educational issues before refocussing on the specific concerns of the language teacher. The best teaching and the most efficient learning may be almost totally undone by the wider social forces which are operating. Wherever there is fear, embarrassment, invidious comparison, boredom or meaninglessness, learning will not flourish for those affected. Even in the same classroom, a genuine breakthrough in reading, for instance, may be undone by contradictory demands in spelling or calligraphy. So much of what we genuinely achieve in teaching is destroyed by the "hidden curriculum." Nothing could be more self-defeating for a profession or for an economy than to destroy so rapidly what it works so energetically to create.

In a remarkable paper on the economics of literacy, Bormuth (1978) points to the inordinate expenditures on reading improvement in contrast to the neglect of writing competence. If we regard literacy as the successful transactions in a society between writers and readers, efficiency may depend *either* on the general level of reading ability *or* on the general intelligibility of the writers. Bormuth identifies the strange social phenomenon in our society which has led us to mythologize reading and to neglect or actively discourage writing. We will not speculate here about the reasons for this phenomenon but simply draw attention to the urgent need to improve the level of writing competence as part of any literacy campaign. Too much of our reading competency, dearly won, is wasted on the attempt to deal with badly written text — from the inanities of officialese to the pretensions of text book authors. Here is another instance where "assumptive blindness" has impaired our common sense in responding to the simple and obvious.

A number of traditional assumptions about childhood, about schooling, and about dependence have obscured our responsibilities as educators, and have delayed our achievement of maturity as a profession. A mature profession educates, informs, and disciplines its own members in the manner of a fraternity rather than a hierarchy. It knows clearly the limits of its own discipline in relationship to contiguous and often interdependent disciplines. It operates in accordance with a clear code either stated or implied, and allows no personal preference to displace that code when there is conflict within the professional context. Each individual practitioner makes his own professional decisions and takes full responsibility for them: passing the buck is almost impossible within a mature profession. Educators have made significant progress in each of these areas, but there are many unresolved problems, some of which impinge directly on the language learner.

A profession is most clearly characterized by the client relationship and it is here that our most damaging conflicts of role arise. Our clients, during childhood, are by nature globally immature and uniquely open to exploitation.

Parents, in transferring their authority, have natural rights in regarding *themselves* as the real clients, especially considering the historical evolution of schooling. We are not paid directly by our clients — the *contractual* nature of the relationship is obscure. Child clients are seldom voluntarily so, and compulsion is generally inconsistent with clienthood. In dealing with large numbers of clients together, we have institutionalized procedures in which the needs of some clients are subverted to the welfare of others. Finally, we have laid aside confidentiality, the pivot of clienthood, in the interests of competition, punishment and control, extrinsic motivation, and accountability. In my opinion, there is no factor in the instructional setting more crucial to literacy learning than the client relationship.

A further complication unique to educators in this respect arises from the peculiar defenselessness of our clients. A special feature of our expertise must lie in the area of advocacy. In order to set up the conditions supportive of healthy language learning, especially in remedial or recovery situations, teachers are likely to find themselves facing a number of pressures and relationships impinging on their clients in ways demanding a fundamentally protective response. To teach is to attempt to maximize the opportunities for clients to learn, and if they are children, to protect them from the exploitative forces which find the powerlessness of childhood an easy mark.

It is often impossible for a teacher to fulfill continuously the conflicting roles of instructor, disciplinarian, and advocate for each child in a large group. Educational systems have the special responsibility of surrounding teachers with necessary support tailored to resolving *these* conflicts.

As teachers we face enormous problems and impediments in serving our clients *as* clients. Perhaps those who laugh off the whole notion as wildly unrealistic have adequate justification, but if this is the case, we must also be hard-headed enough to accept as necessary the massive literacy failure associated with universal schooling since its inception. We must also accept that much of our discussion and research about improving the teaching of language in the school will have purely academic significance. Alternatively, we can face the uniquely difficult problems of our profession constructively and create the unique and ingenious compromises which will be needed if we are to approach mature and efficient professionalism.

## DEVELOPMENTAL LEARNING ENVIRONMENTS

The most formidable arguments against natural and developmental learning of reading and writing are concerned with the *impracticality* of the proposition within the context of schooling. On close examination and in the light of concrete practical rebuttal these arguments turn out to be both circular and also insulting of human nature. On the one hand they point to the traditional difficulty of mastering literacy and the need for intensive remediation of current failures as evidence of the need to make learning ever more easy by controlling vocabulary, phonic progressions and other sub-skill structures. At the same time, and *through* these controls, they make literacy tasks ever more difficult by destroying those strategies by which the young human brain really learns to cope. (Recall Smith's delightful 1973 exposé, "Twelve Easy Ways to make Learning to Read Difficult.")

How *do* young children learn to cope with such immensely complex tasks as oral language and cognitive categorization? We find this out by gentle, non-invasive, descriptive research — by humble observation. Among a dozen exemplars we could take two moving studies such as Dorothy Butler's (1979), *Cushla and Her Books,* or Glenda Bissex's (1980), *GNYS AT WRK.*

Let's look briefly at a few of the strategies used by young children learning in natural ways:

First, they use the complexity built into the human brain to carry out tasks beyond our present competence to describe or understand — and therefore, in any *accurate* way, to teach. They do so largely because the important people in the developmental environment treat that expectation of learning with faith. Babies learning to talk, for instance, for all their bumblings operate in an environment marked not only by trust but by *appreciation.*

Secondly, they observe their environment with intense curiosity, emulating models of what it is to be human with amazing energy, persistence and eye for detail.

Thirdly, they determinedly make sense of their world. Certainly the nature of that sense — those embryonic theories they vigorously construct — varies according to developmental stages, but each theory is centrally sensible and never wholly wrong. Miscue analysis, and even the fascinating speculations of Bettleheim and Zelan (1982) concerning the sense behind children's errors in reading, have helped us to understand the unremitting reasonableness of natural learning.

Fourthly, they use their knowledge of the world and of language to predict both meanings and details in the behavior of those around them. They display an astonishing ability to compensate for gaps in their knowledge and for weaknesses in certain areas of skill by using the knowledge and skill which *is* accessible to them in a task. Applying this to reading, some theorists such as Stanovich (1980) even go so far as to characterize reading as an "interactive compensatory process."

Fifthly, they approximate and take calculated risks judging for themselves what new challenges will be encompassed within the trials of each day.

Sixthly, they monitor their own performance moment by moment, bringing into play the marvellous feedback capacity of the human brain from the earliest age. They develop a "self-improving strategy," comparing their own performance with the models they emulate but seldom being naturally competitive.

Seventhly, they participate actively whenever this is appropriate, enjoying the sense of community in learning. They seem to prefer those activities which make them feel that they are becoming more like other people, more human, more mature.

Eighthly, they practise assiduously at their own pace and at their own level of persistence. Often this self-imposed 'drill' occurs privately and is therefore likely to be overlooked by an observer studying the behavior.

Ninthly, they take risks within easy reach of security. (In Piagetian terms, they move freely between assimilation and accommodation during learning.) Optimally, they behave like a circus trapeze team at practice in the certain knowledge that a safety net is slung below.

Finally, they display in the long run the universal features of organic behavior in pain-avoidance and in pleasure-seeking.

A summary of these characteristics of developmental learners may prove helpful, except that the first quality is difficult to state in any simple terms. Such learning entails:

1. Brain radiating (using complexity from within),
2. Observing and emulating,
3. Making sense,
4. Predicting,
5. Approximating,
6. Self-regulating,
7. Participating,
8. Practising,
9. Risk-taking and "safety-netting", and
10. Pain-avoidance and pleasure-seeking.

## COPING BEHAVIORS AND CONTROLLING TASK DIFFICULTY

Under the most natural conditions of developmental learning the principles listed above are those which children use to maintain a high level of task success, and also those which efficient teachers or helpers use to facilitate the learning of a pupil. Among the least facilitative and most damaging of interventions are those which contradict a number of these principles, and in particular those which shift the inner-directed natural activities to outer-directed dependent ones.

To what extent do the controls upon which we have come to rely in reading and writing reflect these principles? It is difficult to soften the judgement that because they are largely outer-directed, dependence-producing strategies, they tend to breach all of them, at least in spirit. The more that controls of vocabulary and phonics destroy meaning and the other inner-directed strategies, the less likely are children to cope — the less likely it will be that an accurate match will be made between task difficulty and the competencies required for task success. Certainly many children persistently fail no matter how limited the vocabulary of their first "readers" or how few and regular the phonic associations used.

What other alternatives are open to the teacher of reading and writing? If we take each of these principles in turn and regard them as strategies that can be set up for the learner, we find that we are in possession of very powerful procedures to facilitate success. But first, let us be clear that by "naturalizing" the environment of learning — making it reflect more generally and genuinely the true functions of literacy — we make it more possible for children to bring these natural strategies we have described into play from within their own humanness. Before exercising any controls of our own as teachers we need to maximize the opportunities to use *their* abilities to accurately control success levels.

## 1. Brain-radiating

It is not difficult to construct a list of things which induce people to *interact* with the environment — to bring the complexity of their own brains to bear upon the world. At the high level of generality and abstractness which we love to use in teacher training we lump all these factors together under the term "interest" — how *boring* that still sounds.

Among the most important and specific and varied of factors in the context of literacy are the marvellously brain-enticing poems, songs, and stories which make up a great literature at every stage of development. The central fact of literateness is that we are deeply compensated for its troubles and expenses by the memorableness and pricelessness of what is recorded. A literature records those linguistic things which fascinate and delight us. We have no right as teachers to complain of any lack of brain-enticing content from which to teach.

Other factors which entice the brain to display and use its inner complexities are the challenges we see in the world as *solvable problems*. The brain needs problems as the earth needs water, and even a desert can be made to blossom and

bear fruit. Everything new, strange, bright, and beautiful —
and both literature and the world abound in them — entice
the simplest human brain to do what it is designed to do.
(One thinks immediately of Gerard Manley Hopkins or of
Robert Frost.) Using the term in its broadest sense, the brain
is set up to *enjoy*: to perceive, to relate, and to remember.

The first natural control of task difficulty we have at our
disposal, then, is to present language and experiences which
stimulate the natural energies of thinking. Reading material
that is intrinsically boring or worthless is *harder to read* than
material of genuine value. Meanings which are only faint
mimicries of thought, or worse like so many words in a
workbook, are *harder to write* than meanings that the brain
is bursting to express or share.

## 2. Observing and emulating

Developmental learning cannot begin until the learner has
observed the important people in his environment *using* the
desired skill to fulfill their own genuine life purposes (and
without any intention in the first instance to instruct). That
driving motivation we think of in association with babies
learning to run or climb and youngsters mastering their first
two-wheeler bike arises in the hard-to-fool observing brain
which moves right on to emulation.

As literacy teachers we must be observed daily as lovers of
reading and writing — people who actively practise and are
willing to share its mysteries in fulfilling genuine purposes. If
we model reading and writing in this way as a daily part of
our teaching, we will be compulsively emulated. We will
often be surrounded by curious children asking the very
questions about "how you do it" which we want to teach.

Our second natural control, then, is to *display* and *share*
written language which we respect. Never teach from
material which you yourself find boring, patronizing or
worthless. By modelling how we enter into a fascinating text
as readers or as writers we make it *easier* for the children to
cope.

## 3. Making sense

Any procedure which makes a child think that reading

need not make sense, or even that there is something more important than making sense, will make reading and writing harder for children. This, after all, is the heart of the matter — where language and learning form their closest identity. Even in learning phonics or other parts of the word-solving process children should never lose sight of the comprehending purpose.

Our third way of controlling task difficulty, then, is to keep children deeply aware that written language is sensible. If we are going to be uncompromising about *something*, it had better be that. An expectation that a story will hang together and make sense will make that story easier to read.

## 4. Predicting

A unique ability built into the complexity of the human brain is the ability to know most of the time what lies in the next second or two of experience. Often this knowledge of the proximate future is almost exact in its precision — that's why we can drive a car safely under normal circumstances. Language is no exception to this general rule — we are always completing people's sentences for them. And as we read we almost participate with the author in constructing the text.

Two procedures of task control flow from this principle. First, the more predictable the material, the easier it will be to read. The most highly predictable material is something which *that* brain produced before — hence the power of language-experience techniques by which children read what they themselves have written.

Secondly, by actively teaching the strategies of prediction and by providing satisfying opportunities to practise them (as we do in well-designed cloze teaching) we make reading and writing easier for children. Many children become so misinformed about this matter that they think that the teacher thinks that to predict is to cheat — or at least not to "know" or to really "read". They need to be very clear that *all* readers predict — it is not only honest, it's necessary. (Similarly with writing, they need to be clear that all writers edit — they read back their own writing like an outside reader to check how predictable it is even to them.)

## 5. Approximating

Especially in the early stages of any developmental task approximating dominates learning. Getting things *right* is not what matters. The real secret is in getting *better at it*. Early learning is by nature clumsy and unskilled, and this behavior is not only tolerated but appreciated. To disallow approximation, for instance, in learning to discriminate the phonemes of speech would be to produce a speechless generation. We learn complex skills, strategies and processes very slowly and by small degrees, not by knocking off so many more right/wrong bits of knowledge every day.

A further control at our disposal is to provide for and sensitively monitor approximation. (Some people dislike the word "shaping" in this sense but we can certainly see what the behaviorists are talking about.) Progressive approximations over several readings or editings of the same meaningful text, read-along and cloze techniques, and producing the favorite book habit, all provide simple procedures for making reading and writing "I-can-cope" activities. It is a strange paradox that in the approximating procedures we have some of our most subtle and precise strategies of bringing tasks into the compass of struggling learners.

## 6. Self-regulating

Self-correction, or more positively and accurately, self-regulation make reading and writing easier for children in at least three ways. The child who self-corrects is making sense out of the process; he is also freed from undue external correction which we all find punitive; and most importantly, he reads for himself and will be able to do so whether or not he is being checked by someone else. Such a child is free to learn to read through reading and to write by writing — he makes his own teaching points and achieves his own insights.

Once its importance has been recognized by the teacher, self-regulation is not difficult to induce or to teach. Perhaps the most difficult aspect as teacher is to desist from locating and correcting errors, and to discourage persistent correction by competitive peers. Establish the right to self-correction as the first correction within the community of the classroom.

Comfort in self-correction and independent language use

makes reading and writing easier for children. A little thought by the ingenious teacher will suggest many ways by which self-correction may be encouraged and used as a subtle control of coping behavior.

## 7. Participation

A sense of community sustains complex learning. Nothing destroys or perverts it so rapidly as a sense of isolation. (A possible explanation for this surprising insight may be that for human beings isolation is the worst form of punishment.) Even in its most simple forms, genuinely corporate and non-competitive activity proves to sustain learning in powerful ways. Lively unison reading from an enlarged text of lasting impact to the children allows for appropriate approximation and sustains the underconfident learner in a sense of worth. Corporate writing with the teacher or older children acting as scribe may also bring a sense of participant authorship and personal competence. We need to look closely again at our skills in large group teaching, especially to offset the isolating associated with well-intentioned remedial grouping or individualizing.

The most powerful teaching strategies in reading lie between the extremes of reading *by* the teacher (a necessary and joyful experience) and reading *to* the teacher (too often a painful trial which is also grossly wasteful of the precious time of other readers caught in the ring). There are many procedures, reputably researched, for reading *with* children, whether in a large group or in the individual, remedial setting (e.g., McCracken, 1979, and Holdaway, 1979). The listening post has made it possible to use the powerful read-along situation with ease. Many modifications of cloze procedure used in conjunction with read-along or supported reading are bringing new precision and efficiency to the participant situation. Writing may also be supported in participant ways. Many fine procedural examples will be found in the work of Bill Martin and Peggy Brogan (1972), especially those concerned with "innovating on literary structure."

These two controls of copability through participation and through cloze procedures bring the total we have considered so far to eleven.

## 8. Practising

A single introduction of a high impact poem, song, or story presented in an emulative way has the potential to produce hundreds of individual readings in a class of young children. The read-it-again phenomenon which produces for every child a body of favorite books probably accounts for the success of our very early readers and writers more than any other factor. It channels copious quantities of print and written dialect through the language system of any child fortunate enough to encounter such an environment. Each text carries with it both security and familiarity — if not downright affection — in varying degrees for different texts. No text is known by rote, and therefore each entices from the devotee a challenge of decoding in nice relationship to the known and familiar. Both prediction and self-correction are enhanced by the initial model, and approximation normally operates in a healthy progressiveness because this behavior seldom has an audience to pin-prick.

The massive practice which arises from repetition on demand may be turned to subtle precision by the teacher through a process which might be called "repetition by supply." She may control frequency, spacing between repetitions, and spacing between reading *to* and reading *by*. Similar progressions may be seen or contrived in children's preoccupation with a personal writing theme which progresses through rewritings and editings over the course of days or weeks.

Producing the conditions and motivations for repetition on demand together with practice by natural fascination add further controls to the battery of precise procedures available to the developmental literacy teacher.

## 9. Risk-taking and "safety-netting"

It is important that these two ideas be seen as essential parts of the same process. Learners *do* take significant risks, and thereby greatly accelerate their learning, provided they are certain of the safety net — this is, of course, a well-researched, central condition for exploratory play (Ellis, 1973). We know remarkably little of the precise nature and texture of what I have called the "safety net" as it applies to literacy learning. How *do* effective language teachers safety net their pupils? In the usual environment of age-competency testing, of meticulous correction, of open competition and peer embarrassment, it is easy to see that from the learner's point of view there is either no net at all or it is constructed of barbed wire. Let's be clear that under these circumstances no appreciable desirable learning will occur for many children, and psychological bones will be broken.

Safety-netting is not being sentimentally kind to underconfident kids, nor is it deciding cynically that nothing much more can be done without making things worse. Whatever the subtle qualities of this teaching skill may be in classroom or clinic, it must certainly rank among the supreme abilities of the effective teacher. It is my point of view — or perhaps I should say hunch — that essentially it entails the ability to set up a true client relationship with every pupil as discussed above.

The teacher who is very skilled, then, has a further range of techniques for making reading and writing successful experiences — the techniques by which the failing or underconfident learner may be persuaded that it is safe to take risks.

*10. Pain-avoidance and pleasure seeking*

There is little point in laboring such topics as reinforcement contingencies or the permissible uses of punishment: the facts are clear, the research has been out in abundant conclusiveness for decades, and further evidence will not significantly change the issues. It should be said, however, that we are rapidly increasing our knowledge of how to make learning to read and write both pleasant and efficient. This is thanks in no small measure to the growing body of fine children's authors and illustrators, and to the publishers who present them without instructional pre-processing. If we wish to make literacy more pleasurable most rapidly, we may begin in no better way than in making connections between children and the literature addressed to them honestly as developing human beings rather than as objects of instruction.

Here we could return to that set of techniques and those patterns of organization which make it possible for children to select a large proportion of their reading material from a rich and varied body of books. Individualized Reading and Sustained Silent Reading have a reputable history in theory, research and practice. Impediments to their wider application are becoming less compelling in the eighties. Certainly, we can help children to cope and to thrive in reading and writing by using this eminently sensible body of attitudes and practices which trust children to select, act upon, and share what is relevant to them in written language (Veatch, 1968; Barbe, 1975; Holdaway, 1980).

## SUMMARY OF COPING PROCEDURES

As we summarize the alternatives we have examined to the controls of vocabulary, phonic progression, and sub-skill mastery to which we have increasingly turned to solve the literacy problem, it may be salutory to ask three questions of each principle. Is it sustained by both research and good sense? Does it ask too much of the teacher who has to do the job? In economic terms, will it be expensive to implement in comparison with current materials?

1. High impact presentation of high impact materials,
2. Genuine modelling of joyful literacy by the teacher,
3. Demanding sense,
4. Encouraging prediction,
5. Using predictable materials at lower levels,
6. Using children's own "publishing",
7. Providing for approximation,
8. Developing self-correction and self-regulation,
9. Increasing corporate teaching strategies,
10. Reading with, read-along, controlled cloze procedures,
11. Inducing repetition on demand,
12. Favorite book practices,
13. Safety-netting, and
14. Self-selection.

# CHAPTER 3

# Literacy Programs in the Eighties

In the light of the foregoing discussion of stability and change as reflected in research trends, and bearing in mind the formidable enabling conditions required for learning in school, the following brief summary of current trends may help to clarify our concerns. Each of these trends reflects a considerable international consensus and I will not attempt to acknowledge sources unless there is some special reason for doing so.

## 1. Learning leads teaching

Theory and research in the last decade has moved increasingly towards an emphasis on development and learning rather than on teaching, and the practical implications have begun to be worked out in pockets of change within rigidly instructional systems. This movement could be characterized as a radical shift of emphasis from content to process in the area of language learning, i.e., from items to be taught and remembered to strategies for linguistic action, from concern for the surface structures of language alone to concern for the making of meanings at a deep level through manipulating the code.

An important consequence of this emphasis will be a greater concern for the environment of learning and for control of the conditions of learning rather than for techniques of instruction alone. The advent of the mini-computer displays potential for accelerating this change of emphasis to learning, exploring and functioning in language.

2. *Learning to read through reading* (and to write through writing).

A greater awareness of the vital part played by genuine language *use* in the learning of language strategies is leading to a new interest in programs which are based on functioning, such as individualized reading, sustained silent reading, thematic study, shared book experience, language experience, and related language and arts programs.

More recently, this emphasis has become apparent in explorations in the teaching of writing (Graves, 1983). Writing for a genuine audience, and special provision for the strategies of editing, seem to be the new priorities. Basal reading programs and traditional approaches to writing and spelling do not lend themselves well to these developmental principles, but no doubt the publishers will make some panic changes of terminology if not of content — here comes the Basal Language Program!

(Frank Smith [1982] is professing a change of conviction to the effect that we do not learn to write by writing but by reading. Personally, as I have indicated above, I believe that literacy transactions display functional integrity — to a significant extent reading and writing are the same process. The copious and compelling research concerned with predictive functioning, with the cloze phenomenon, and with story schema and discourse analysis, would seem to support the contention that the reader participates with the author in "writing" the text just as the writer participates with readers through the reading part of his competence, i.e., he tests the surface structure of what he is writing *as a reader* in order to write.)

3. *Quality literature versus instructional materials*

The sanity of using an open literature at the centre of the instructional program in reading and writing is being increasingly accepted. At the same time, criticism of instructional materials, which have so often been denatured as literature, becomes more penetrating. Properly articulated with points 1 and 2 above, we have the basis of a literacy program in which the dominating activities will be genuine reading, writing, talking, and listening together with the exploration of meanings in the related arts.

The need to familiarize children with the *written* dialect, first through the ear and across the tongue, has profoundly enriched and extended language-experience techniques. A program based on the immediate utility of real life language enriched by copious experience of memorable story, poem and song would meet many of our most urgent priorities in theory.

### 4. Whole text study versus the study of snippets

A growing body of research and classroom exploration now centres on the influence of whole text awareness, from the earliest stages, both on the processes of comprehension and on the minutiae of decoding. The learner's growing projection of story or text schema in anticipatory hypotheses, and his or her growing ability to perceive text structure (assimilation and accommodation) constitute essential strategies not only in comprehension but also in word perception.[3] These strategies are also essential in the generation of writing, especially copious, completed writing which drives on through beginning and middle to consummation. Many teachers are exploring the generative power of "innovating on literary structure" (Bill Martin and Peggy Brogan, 1972).

### 5. Psycholinguistic insights
a. The return to meaning:

The last twenty years has seen a growing concentration on code-emphasis approaches. However, psycholinguistic research, which redefines reading in terms of meaning, has been chipping at the phonics monolith for some years with increasing success. A more accurate view of reading process emphasizes the crucial input of the reader — the "inside-out" nature of reading has now been thoroughly documented. By implication, any activity which increases awareness of meanings — generates, explores or clarifies meanings

— such as do the related arts, can be seen to support both reading and writing deeply. The function of related arts activity in the literacy program goes beyond motivation (our previous excuse for sporadic activity) to the very centre of the transactions. The arts are crucial to the program, not peripheral.

b. Prediction and cloze procedures:

Perhaps the most startling and conclusive contribution of psycholinguistic research has been to display the dominance of predictive processes in every aspect of reading and writing. A whole new technology of teaching is growing up around so-called "cloze procedures" but this technology has not yet been clearly reflected in published programs. A combination of read-along and oral cloze procedures forms one of the most powerful ways of inducing successful reading and learning, especially in the recovery context, and can be adapted to induce written responses.

A danger in this area is that early research with cloze was associated with testing reading and determining readability. Although the deletion frequencies commonly used in those contexts may produce statistically reliable results, they cannot be recommended for teaching. Considerable research and exploration is required in the use of cloze procedures to achieve learning objectives.

c. Self-regulation:

A strong body of research points to the importance of self-regulating behavior from the beginnings of reading and writing. Although this is a complex area of research in which much has yet to be determined with specificity, the corrective tradition in the teaching of language has been put to serious question. Self-correction or confirmation can be seen as an indispensable part of the hypothesis/test strategy which governs reading efficiency.

d. Syntactic clarity:

An intuitive awareness of syntactic operations during reading has been shown to underlie competence.

Word-recognition in real reading occurs under the strong influence of syntactic expectations and maintains a high syntactic coherence. Word-recognition practices which exclude the operation of syntax seem highly questionable on this ground alone. The syntactical patterns of written language should become highly familiar to young readers, not through analysis which destroys intuitive rapidity and confuses, but through constant meaningful use. Cloze teaching facilitates this learning.

e. Problem-solving:

In contrast to the traditional emphasis on memory and the pre-teaching of vocabulary, it has been shown that successful readers use a hypothesis/test strategy in solving textual problems. This entails bringing meaningful expectations to the text, sampling detail, hypothesizing, and confirming. Attention to graphophonic cues occurs as a *part* of that process. So much of our teaching in reading and spelling is concerned with items smaller than the sentence that we are actively discouraging the use of the meaning-dominated strategies most typical of language.

f. Miscue analysis:

Descriptive techniques of monitoring and evaluation such as miscue analysis and its many variants are replacing normative instruments at least to some extent. There is great need for improving general teacher competence in modifying and applying these techniques. The analysis of retellings, which have tended to be neglected in practical application, would seem to deserve much more attention particularly in light of insights from discourse analysis and in terms of the need for longitudinal evaluation (Goodman, 1965; Goodman and Burke, 1972, 1980).

## 6. Developmental considerations

A growing awareness of natural stages of development in reading and writing is at last beginning to influence the teaching of literacy. In particular, a complete rethinking about early literacy is under way. Traditional assumptions about readiness and pre-reading have been largely discredited and are being replaced by a more accurate perception of emergent literacy.

A deeper understanding of Piagetian principles is pointing to the enrichment and normalizing of stages of development in contrast to the traditional concern for acceleration through stages.

The natural model of successful developmental learning outside the context of formal instruction has at last attracted serious attention and has provided a highly generative set of ideas, particularly in reshaping early schooling. This is especially important for literacy which is so closely related to the most incontestably efficient learning we know. As indicated earlier, research affirmation of this model provides one of our most reliable sources of stability.

### 7. The "literacy" concept

In contrast to the traditional separation of reading and writing within instructional programs, modern research has displayed the integrity of learning to deal with print. Increasingly, programs will embody this integral association between reading and writing, speaking and listening.

Some deep thinking is called for concerning our traditional neglect of writing in contrast to our almost hysterical concern with reading. It may be that in the industrial society of the past it was of vital importance to inform people and instruct them in what they were to do, while it was of dubious value, or even dangerous, for the generality to write well. This is certainly not true of the age into which we are moving. Writing ability will carry a bonus in ordinary living.

The typewriter is a fascinating instrument for the creation of writing. Competent typing displays that incomparable automaticity we see in mature language functioning such as talking. In general, the machine has been used for copying rather than for composing, but it has great potential if mastered sufficiently early. However, the mini-computer and word-processor, because they carry the competence to store and edit, represent a breakthrough for composition, and young children seem to have remarkable facility in learning to handle computers. (Perhaps, because it is not yet in the syllabus!) Computer competence will be a vital general skill in the future, and that competence displays the essential features of writing. It is likely that we will shortly find ourselves in a society of young writers, or at least in a society in which the ability to write for everyday and work purposes will carry a mighty bonus. The term "computer literacy" has crept into our vocabulary in the last decade. It embodies much more than a slick metaphor.

## 8. *Longitudinal evaluation*

There is a growing and well-founded professional uneasiness about current testing techniques, although the temptations of computer processing in the area of evaluation and accountability strongly support current normative procedures. The movement towards descriptive, developmental, and longitudinal procedures in research is influencing classroom practice and providing the instruments for reliable procedures of monitoring individual progress more acceptably. The essence of these procedures lies in longitudinal and developmental analysis and assessment. Dated examples of actual linguistic behavior are filed for each individual, who is then tracked according to his or her individual progress rather than in comparison with group norms. This file takes the form of dated writing samples, records of reading in the form of modified miscue procedures (including retellings and preferably recorded on a continuous tape for each individual), anecdotal observations made by the teacher, and cloze probes from normal reading rather than from tests.

Such procedures serve the needs of individual learners with more justice and precision than do standardized tests, which lack the developmental and diagnostic dimensions. They help to maintain essential confidentiality, provide sensitive measures of approximation learning, and form a sound basis for accountability, especially to parents and to the learners themselves. Standardized tests will continue to have a proper function, but that function can be fulfilled by a single test given annually.

## 9. Corporate learning

There is a growing interest in the social dimensions of literacy and of learning. Although individualization remains a central *objective*, the most efficient conditions for its achievement, especially in language, involve social motivation and action. The most powerful language learning situations involve all children in a group or class in the healthy interactions of a community and linguistically active for a majority of the time. The most hardy learning takes place within supportive social groups characterized by a lack of competition or invidious comparison. The traditional emphases on hearing reading, individual seat-work, ardent phonication, and the marking of written work beyond the context of effort, have all been shown to be both counter-productive and unnecessary. Shared Book Experience procedures, in particular, provide a new body of techniques for corporate activity in language.

## 10. Reading recovery or literacy emancipation

There is a strengthening movement away from the medical model which has so unduly influenced the area of learning disabilities and remedial education in the last twenty years. Problems in the mastery of literacy skills are being seen as demanding the normalization of developmental processes and the clarification of cognitive confusion. The problem learner is now being perceived in terms of conditions within the instructional setting rather than as disabled or "sick" because of some hypothetical condition within himself. This brings proper control and responsibility back to the teacher as teacher rather than as therapist, and demands educational rather than medical, or medically inspired, manipulation.

Establishing and maintaining successful linguistic functioning becomes the central educational challenge. Dependence upon vocabulary or phonic controls to achieve a match between learner and materials or tasks has proved both inefficient and ill-founded. Psycholinguistic and developmental procedures provide extremely delicate control over difficulty in materials or tasks: read-along techniques, cloze procedures in teaching, predictability controls of material, the "favorite book syndrome" of massive repetition on demand, corporate problem-solving in text, and many other procedures provide virtually complete control in establishing and maintaining success. For instance, if we have a twelve-year-old who tests at seven years for reading, it is no longer necessary to attempt the impossible and find a text at the seven year vocabulary level which will be mature enough for his interests. We can determine his interests and find a fascinating text at the twelve or thirteen year level with which to begin a recovery program. Through participant reading with oral cloze involving deletions at about the 1:10 level, we can begin with a fascinating experience of success and satisfaction. Alternatively, we have four or five other techniques to establish or maintain success.

This is not the place for a lengthy discussion of recovery procedures, but with our current knowledge we are on the verge of a genuine breakthrough in this area. Only our prejudices, our precedents, and our false assumptions about the nature of language processes stand in the way of general amelioration of the literacy scandal.[4]

This highly simplified consideration of trends for the eighties leaves many arguable questions to one side. However, it can be said that we are now constructing, for the first time since Huey (1908), a coherent and inter-related body of insights which transcends the jumble-box thinking of eclecticism and is productive of clear educational objectives. This is an exciting time for literacy. Certainly we have the basis for both stability and change. And a large area for continuing research, classroom exploration, and healthy debate.

# CHAPTER 4

# Developmental Teaching of Literacy

We have explored major trends in teaching literacy for the early eighties with special emphasis on the developmental model. Our aims in analyzing the environments of literacy learning were constructive rather than being merely deprecatory of current inadequacies, although we found strong reasons for urgent change in some surprising areas. Fundamentally, we are attempting to find positive, workable alternatives in those areas which call for change. So far we have emphasized learning and the learner, especially the learner operating under optimal developmental conditions in "natural" learning largely outside the scope of direct instruction. What are the implications for *teaching* in a developmentally orientated classroom setting?

Seen from this perspective the teacher has four major roles displaying rather different, and certainly less intrusive, priorities than we normally think of in the context of instruction.

## 1. Establishing a favorable environment

This should be an environment in which the conditions of learning we have discussed are maximized. For our purposes it will be one in which literacy is of high human value, purposeful, inviting, functional, and associated with deep satisfactions. It will be supplied with a great variety of print but in particular it will be a virtual storehouse of literature relevant to the age group. An area for relaxed reading would be an advantage as would the space required for shared reading, drama and dance.

### 2. *Inducing or modelling reading and writing*
Teachers should read and write to and with the children every day. They must be able to display what it is like to be joyfully literate and expect to be emulated and appealed to to share their skill.

### 3. *Establishing language in action*
On the developmental basis of learning-through-doing the teacher must get the children reading and writing, listening and talking as actively as good order will allow. Central to this activity will be the exploration of meanings in the real world, in literature, and in the related arts. A good language period will be one in which most of the children will be cognitively and linguistically active most of the time.

### 4. *Providing instruction*
a.  Demonstrate literacy (implied by 2 above).
b.  Induce healthy strategies in participant ways. Work as a community to solve problems, especially those of print. Be invitational of suggestions and actively encourage prediction. Develop techniques of response which allow you to be positive in over ninety percent of your feedback. Reward risk-taking, self-correction, and discovery. Both oral and written cloze techniques will assist you to achieve this high level of participation and success.
c.  Clarify process. Progressively share with the children as you read and write how you *really* do it. Encourage the children to develop their own explanations of how to do things and what goes on in their heads as they attempt to read and write.
d.  Give help rather than advice. When the children are working independently let them know you are ready to give them the actual help they ask for but encourage them to have a go at answering their own question (such as how to spell a particular word) and praise the

positive aspects of their attempts.

e. Monitor growth on an individual, long-term basis rather than a comparative one. Evaluate longitudinally and continuously, keeping individual files which contain chiefly either actual examples of reading and writing or meticulously descriptive notes on actual behavior. Be careful to date everything in the file.

Such an analysis of roles is not very helpful without exemplification and we will now look closely into a classroom or two. However, read within the context of the earlier chapters, the suggested changes of role from the heavily instructional model should stand out fairly clearly.

Setting up a developmental *learning* environment in the primary grades is not difficult — it is just unusual and unpopular. The three basic requirements are: modelling or demonstration of the desired skill in genuine ways (e.g., baby grows in a rich environment of oral language use), participation invited and rewarded (e.g., the baby begins approximating use of the language), and independent, self-motivated practice at a level selected by the brain of the learner (e.g., the baby engages in practice burblings whether or not there is an audience). For reading and writing these three conditions could be stated as:

| 1. Reading *to* | 2. Reading *with* | 3. Reading *by* |
|---|---|---|
| Writing *for* or *to* | Writing *with* (scribing) | Writing *by* |
| INPUT | INPUT/OUTPUT | OUTPUT |

Time and equipment are organized to provide for and enrich these three types of activity. In a block of language and related arts time of say an hour and a half, Section 3, natural, developmental practice, will be most time-consuming: the teacher will spend about forty minutes in activities 1 and 2, and the children will spend about fifty minutes in activity 3, while the teacher interacts naturally to provide help, sustain activity, act as V.I.P. audience, observe and note, and teach individuals or small groups.

The Input Time, when the teacher is the centre of activity, will normally involve the whole class as a community of learners covering a wide range of levels corporately. The materials and procedures will be of such a kind as to allow children to engage in participant learning at their own levels. Above all, this is a time for pleasure in language, and the teacher radiates enjoyment and skill. The children wish to emulate and participate, and they find it possible to do so at different levels but each coping according to the principles outlined in Chapter 2.

This time may be divided in a number of ways suited to the teacher and the learning objectives in mind. A pattern which has proved very popular among teachers will be exemplified in the classroom descriptions which follow. The pattern may be summarized as follows:

1. *Tune-in*. Poems, songs, chants, dances, etc.
2. *Old Favorite*. Story re-read on demand — often enlarged.
3. *Learning About Language*. Very brief "skill" lesson.
4. *New Story*. Normally one every day.
5. *Independent Reading and Activity*. Often involving related arts.

The Output Time should be as unstructured as possible, allowing for personal choice of materials, level of operation, and type of activity. Naturally, much of the activity which is forthcoming during this activity output time will have been stimulated, initiated, or demonstrated in the preceding participant activity with the teacher.

*KINDERGARTEN OR GRADE 1* (Emergent Literacy)

Suppose the children have been at school for about six weeks, some routines have been established, and there is already a stock of loved poems, songs, and stories, some in large print, with which the children are very familiar. The class of twenty-five children ranges from youngsters who have seldom had a story read to them before coming to school to those who are extremely book-sophisticated; from those whose spoken dialect is distant from the formal language of school to those who already display two or three registers including the dialect of book language; from a few whose first language is not English to those who have explored very special written language effects in shared literature and song at home. There may even be one or two children who, in an important sense, can read and write. The class is a normal cross-section of many communities.

The children know the routine and gather expectantly around the teacher who has everything needed within reach for snappy continuity. There is a collection of favorite poems, songs, and stories in enlarged print; an easel for displaying enlarged books and charts; a blackboard or felt pen to facilitate writing on the spot; the new book for today (possibly displayed before the lesson), and a chair. The session begins and proceeds something like the following:

1. *Tune-in.* Enjoyment of favorite poems, songs and jingles, displayed on enlarged text and chosen by request. There is likely to be a new piece for the day or a new activity, such as actions, for an old familiar favorite.

We begin at a good pace, the children participating in unison. Some of the pieces have finger or body actions. Some are suitable for part-taking. The children can all see the text and either the teacher or one of the children points, using a pointer so as not to obscure the text. Today we zip through six or seven pieces with full-blooded intonation, natural speech rhythms, and quick pace (no time for messing about between pieces). The real favorite is the song from yesterday:

> *Love somebody?*
>
> *Yes I do!* (3 times)
>
> *And I hope somebody*
>
> *Loves me too.*

Today we talk about those we love and decide to change the song and put in the substitutes — Mummy, Daddy, Grandma, puppy, etc. Then we begin to write one of the new verses. The children have already worked out that it can't be "Love Mummy?" because they have sung it; so we start writing "Love my Mummy?" We ask the children for help in spelling "Mummy" and notice the funny double em in passing. (Tomorrow we'll probably change the "hope" to something more suitable to "Mummy", like "know" or "I'm sure" — good chance to introduce those nasty basics right early on.)

2. *Old Favorite*. Today the children choose *The Gingerbread Man* which they have enjoyed in the enlarged format three times before. Today we use cardboard masks or a variable exposure mask to identify and talk about the words "fast" and "faster". The children use the masks to locate the recurring items in the story, and suggest other words which behave in the same way — "slow", "high", and "fat". After the story has been enjoyed we suggest that some may like to hear it again in the listening post later in the day. We also suggest that this would be a good story for us to act out sometime. (A few children will probably attempt to do so freely in the output session later.)

3. *Learning about Language*. This is a very brief period in which something useful in decoding the new story today will be taught, and/or something previously introduced will be consolidated, e.g., a new alphabet book (we already have five), selecting initial letters which begin personal names, an "I Spy" game, etc.[5]

Today we recapitulate and further clarify the concept "word". We look for big words and little words in the familiar *Gingerbread Man*, and some of our own names, listening, looking, and comparing. After one of the "reading" children mentions the idea of "more letters" we do a little counting of letters, but don't make a great issue of it — our target concept at the moment is "word". The notion will be picked up again and used in the forms "one word" and "two words" in exploring the new story.

4. *New Story*. This is the highlight of the day as a rule, and although natural participation will be induced and encouraged, we will allow nothing to interfere with the fun and flow of the story.

We choose another of Bill Martin's *Instant Readers* — a

number are already in our library of favorites, especially, *When It Rains It Rains*, and *Monday, Monday, I Like Monday*, which were introduced during the first week at school. This one, *Brown Bear, Brown Bear, What Do You See?* is likely to become a special favorite if past experience means anything. This year there is a large version available and we are lucky to have obtained a copy.[6] We begin reading, enjoying the vivid art and taking a more leisurely pace in this instance. The children soon intuit the structure — a delightfully predictable pattern with a new animal and a new color on each page:

*Yellow duck, yellow duck, what do you see?*

*I see a blue horse looking at me.*

The children begin to chime in with gusto almost from the beginning. When we finish the first reading, we briefly refer to the "two words" — a color and an animal. We find them in the text. On the second reading, which is demanded with more than mild pleadings, we take special note of those two changing words, always in the same place and locatable by all but the two or three children for whom the word "word" doesn't yet mean constantly "word".[7]

In a day or two all of the children will be able to read the book confidently with what Bill Martin calls "joyous familiarity." The familiarity comes from two sources: in the language-using mind of each child there are patterns which mesh with the predictable patterns of the book; and *all* of the children will return to the text many times in individual or group settings (with someone role-playing teacher) gaining what I have called "massive repetition on demand."

5. *Independent Reading, Writing and Related Arts.* There is a warm glow in the group as we complete the new story. The children are now well and truly turned on to language and meanings. They are ready for a wide variety of activities in related language and art. There has been a sufficiently stimulating input to generate a range of preoccupations differing in process and level of difficulty. The environment is ready with all of the favorite books and poems, some of them

produced and illustrated by the children but scribed by the teacher. Materials for exploratory writing are available in a range of formats (One child even *prefers* a lead pencil to all the bright colors — perhaps he thinks that a more proper medium for real writing.) The listening post is ready to function with a variety of favorite tape-book sets available. Art materials have been prepared in one corner for the inevitable colored animal book that will be put together in the next few days. The teaching materials we use are available for children to role-play teacher with a voluntary group of four or five who have worked out their own democratic process for who plays teacher today. Small, spirit-duplicated books of popular pieces — text only — are available for illustrating and personalizing before being taken off home to display prowess. (All the parents know what we are up to because we have sent home a couple of explanatory letters warning that these early readings are as precious and often as clumsy as the first words a baby speaks.)

The children spend about forty minutes in these activities at this stage. Most undertake three or four different activities. For some there is a little ritual they like to follow, such as reading a "big book" and pointing with precision, writing a "story" with only semblances of letter forms, playing with alphabet blocks, and finally listening to a story or two in the listening post. Other children will persevere with a single task for all or most of the time with the odd scatty day in between. Others again seem to cooperate in fairly stable groups in similar tasks.

In order to keep track of all this behavior we keep realistic longitudinal records for each of the children. This includes a personal 60 minute tape on which we periodically record part of a favorite story volunteered to be read with some pride. Each segment is dated as are the examples of art and "writing" we collect.

Although we teach in a very energetic manner during the Input Time, we are very relaxed during the Output Time and often refreshed by the opportunity to observe and help in such enthusiastic practice and learning. We enjoy the opportunity to react with and think about individual children and make plans about materials and techniques we will use in the future. The children often display common preoccupations and pockets of interest arise around which we scheme thematic experiences. The children often help in this way to decide which books, poems, and songs to select for the next few days and their natural strivings to read, write and understand indicate where a proper emphasis may be placed and a progression constructed for future teaching.

We try to think creatively about those "basic skills" which seem to be regarded as the bricks and mortar of reading and writing at least by the great program makers. As we see evidence of learning in the more natural environment, the metaphors we begin to think in become organic rather than structural — strategies, purposes and processes growing and being nurtured rather than edifices of brick and concrete being built, and problem-solving brains comprehending their world with our help rather than cognitive poverty being enriched by gifts from our knowledge and our curriculum. It is a rather humbling experience but a genuinely rewarding one to realize that we don't *have* the skills to build into their competencies or lack of them — the skills are growing naturally and observably within them.

This doesn't mean going overboard about letting the children do whatever they will. On the contrary, there is much more of a call for special knowledge and a greater responsibility to make decisions and to plan. For instance, we see clearly that a few basic function words make up the largest bulk of reading and writing and that having early automatic control over those words will greatly facilitate our early readers and writers. But it is now our task to focus on those words in natural rather than boring and threatening ways, and we puzzle about how to teach them more efficiently, in a way that will not jeopardize automaticity, by procedures which will not produce anxiety and self-consciousness in even a small proportion of our class.

The children already collect and decorate some of their favorite words from the literature like commercial artists might do. They include fascinating words like "lion", "Goldilocks" and "troll". But who would ever pick "went", "want", or "what" to decorate their inner landscape? We think of the experiences of reading and writing which arose from Bill Martin's version of *The Teeny Tiny Woman*, and how the children displayed no difficulty with "me" and "my" and "take it". (We resist the temptation for a sneaky test of those words out of context — our objective is for children to read and write early and with ease, and they are already doing that. Criterion fulfilled.) We do keep a record of basic words, letter-sound associations, and special features of print which arise as we enjoy the literature and our writing, and we use a range of focus techniques, especially in using enlarged print, to highlight a small corpus of important concepts or items each day.

Although we don't test words isolated from context because such a practice seems to breach almost every principle of developmental learning, we do observe children dealing with words in new contexts, cut up and reorder very familiar sentences, match isolated words back into a standing context, reduce and expand sentences, and use basic structures to modify and make our own "literature". Following the dozens of individual and group readings which sprang from the ten minutes we spent initially in sharing *The Teeny Tiny Woman*, we used the old rhebus idea which used to be used generations ago. We use a melodious little bell sparingly to call the class to general attention, so we wrote on the blackboard:

*Give me my*

and asked, "Can anyone do what that tells you to do?" There were several volunteers. Jim is chosen and fetches the bell without a word. (This soundless communication will be very useful as the days go by.) Now we wrote:

*Give my*  *to Valerie.*

Jim chose a volunteer who carried out the instruction. Now we wrote:

*Valerie, give it to me.*

Valerie obliged. Now we all looked closely at the text to find and explain the difference between "me" and "my". In the clarity of the present context all of the children seem to understand, but we know that in an hour or two or tomorrow several of the children who are still vague about the concept "word" would not be able to perform in this way. That is natural, too, in development. The main thing is that we are achieving real life literacy at different rates for all of the children, and we have added to rather than thrown out the wisdom of the past.

These children may not be receiving a "readiness program" or appropriate "pre-reading activities" (if there *are* any which are not associated with written dialect and with print): however, they are learning to behave in literate ways. When they move on into Grade 1 or further, they will carry within them winning strategies for readers and writers. They are more than ready, they are under way.

## EARLY READING AND WRITING — A GRADE 1 OR 2 SETTING

The natural model is at its most powerful at this point of stress where the real nitty-gritty of reading instruction is expected to be undertaken. From the point of view of optimal learning, stress is the last thing we need. For too many children, failure at this level, i.e., failure to meet the external criteria, marks the beginning of a slide into years of misery and confusion from which it will be difficult to recover even with the best of remedial provisions.

At this level we will structure time in essentially the same way as we did at the Kindergarten level. The differences will be subtle changes in the sophistication of learning strategies and of teaching procedures. At the Emergent Stage there may be little coordinated attention to the actual visual detail of print although an early awareness of directional conventions

appears to be very important.[8] An awareness of the conven-
tion of spaces begins to clarify the concept of "a word" and a
one-to-one match between spoken and printed words begins
to be made in very familiar material. However, these very
young readers rely heavily on their knowledge of language
and the world, aided greatly by intuiting the predictable
structures which usually characterize stories, poems and
songs which young children enjoy.

At the second, the Early Reading Stage — what has been
thought of as Beginning Reading — something very different
is expected and something different again is likely to happen
for children who cope. It is expected that attention to visual
detail will become meticulous and that this attention to
graphic features conjoined with phonics (attention to grapho-
phonic cues) will lead to accurate word recognition and real
reading will then begin.

However, rather than radically changing the cues to which
they attend, many fortunate children will refine and build on
their earlier strategies without developmental discontinuity.
They will begin to integrate or put together information from
several cue systems *including* visual detail. This allows them
to approach the perceptual certainty (surface level accuracy)
without losing the meaningfulness which is the very epitome
of the true reader (deep structure comprehension). It is the
determination to write which seems to generate insights
about the relationships between letters and sounds — at least
among the precocious or earliest readers and writers.[9]

During the Early Literacy phase children need to develop a
flexible multi-cued hypothesis/test strategy as they come to
grips with the confusing orthography of English. This "It
could be/yes it is" strategy invites the learner to explore
several different and important aspects of orthography at the
same time without losing touch with the central task of
achieving meaning. It is very difficult to learn and know how
to use rules or generalizations which are unreliable — and
nobody would call the principles of English spelling reliable.
Learning English phonics and spelling is more a matter of
ordering, ranking and cross-referencing *tendencies or
options*. The integration of different cue systems, of which
meaning is the most indispensable, allows exceptions and

peculiarities to be both tolerated and handled. (No one can read the word "tear" with certainty unless meaning brings something to the eye.)

At this stage there may be a distinct and healthy slowing down of response pace — a tendency to pause, to puzzle, to re-run, and to check. Such deliberation may color responses by a lack of pleasing fluency but it should never be allowed to suppress the natural, meaning-seeking, predictive strategies evident at the Emergent Literacy stage. When we respond to the "errors" or "miscues" children must make as they tangle with word-recognition and spelling, we should be considering the *nature and quality* of the miscues rather than simple rightness and wrongness.[10] Nor should we forget the comforting universality of approximation in all successful natural learning.

In developmental learning continuity is healthy and good while discontinuity is usually bad and to be avoided wherever possible. We need to teach the strategies of reading and writing in a manner which provides for continuous refinement and consistency without sudden contradictions or discontinuities. In Early Reading and Writing, i.e., Stage Two in literacy development, we need to continue and build on the enjoyment of language and meaning-making which so deeply characterizes Emergent Literacy. Furthermore, we should avoid teaching anything which must be contradicted or displaced in later grades. This includes such general concepts as that reading is recognizing or saying words, such narrowly wrong advice as "sound it out", such confusing metaphors as "the sounds letters make" (they are all and always silent), or such rules as are wrong more often than they are right, e.g., "When two vowels go walking, the first one does the talking."

Building on the Kindergarten structure, let's sample what may happen in a typical hour and a half in the early primary grades.

*Tune-in:* Six or seven poems, songs, chants and jingles at a fast clip and using enlarged text. Today we introduce a new poem in book form, *Fire! Fire! Said Mrs. McGuire* — another Bill Martin Instant Reader. We all enjoy the way the rhymes are made with people's names and realize that we could make a poem like this ourselves, using our own names. Later in the afternoon we will get together and begin making our *Fire! Fire!* book. (See below under "Independent Activity and Related Arts.")

*Old Favorites:* The children choose *There Was an Old Lady Who Swallowed a Fly* and read it this time rather than sing it. They have illustrated a large version made of sturdy paper and hand-written by the teacher. The "of course" at the very end has been designed in large, colorful, explosive letters like advertising copy (and that's another nasty piece of English orthography handled delicately rather than coarsely at an early age over the dead bodies of vocabulary controllers).

For our own teaching purposes we choose next *The Thing from Somewhere* by Carol Blackburn and Libby Handy, and published in "Big Book" format. There are no complaints — this is always a welcome choice. This little piece of science fiction for young children has a comfortably predictable structure with a rising temperature or tension through frustration and misery to explosive resolution. The children have been fascinated by the bold print design and this has been reflected in some of their own writing.

Today we home in on one theme from the book, the cans and can'ts of animal behavior. The frog can leap, and croak and swim, but he can't walk, or fly or bark. We turn this into a language-experience personalization, scribing the children's suggestions, "I can . . ." "I can't . . ." on a large sheet of paper pinned to the easel. There is useful discussion about whether *we* can fly, or whether it is airplanes that fly. The children like the suggestion that they make their own "I Can — I Can't" books.

*New Story:* We choose a story in normal sized print from *The Sounds of Laughter* by Bill Martin and Peggy Brogan. We gain participation and the opportunity for our major teaching objectives by using the "oral cloze" technique in which we hesitate with an invitational look and tone before the word we want the children to predict.

The Funny Old Man and the Funny Old Woman
                                by Martha Barber.

*A funny old man and a funny old woman*

*sat by the fire one night.*

*"Funny old man," the old woman said,*

*"I don't know what to --.*

*When I went to the barn to milk the ---*

*the funny old cow wouldn't ---."*

The children delight in the illustrations which, in reading the story to the children, we use to confirm or reinforce predictions rather than to arouse motivation beforehand.

*The funny old man scratched his ----*
(no child would suggest "hand" as some
would if engaged in flashcard drills).

*"I know what to do," he said.*

*"Take her to town to see Doctor -----*

*and bring her home in the morning.*

*That's what you -- when the --- ---- ---."*

*"But she's out in the woodshed lying ----.*

*How will you take the cow to town*

*and bring her back in --- -------?"*

*"If she can't walk," said the funny old man,*

*"I'll push her in the ----------- if I can,"*

We stop at "wheelbarrow" with an invitational lilt of intonation. Different children suggest "cart", "pram", "wheelbarrow", "buggy" and "sledge". Each of these responses is received with a warm and genuine comment such as, "I like that!" or "Yes! Could be." By using this oral cloze procedure we are able to give very positive feedback quite honestly to every response — senseless responses simply don't occur, wrong responses don't occur, negative feedback from the teacher, then, doesn't need to occur.

Every child in the class is cognitively active in problem-solving and each has an excellent chance of approval from the teacher. We begin to *induce* the hypothesis/test strategy without giving any instructions and without confusing a single child. If you want high level responses, set up sensible situations.

Now we begin to reduce uncertainty further before moving to a decision and certainty. The lad who suggested "sledge" had allowed his brain to be seduced away from syntax by the search for a possibly pushable farm vehicle. "Is there any of those suggestions that can't possibly fit?" we ask. Somebody says, "Sledge, 'cos you go *on* a sledge not *in* it."

At this stage we home in on the grapho-phonic information, in this case the purely visual or configurational features. "No this is a very *big* word, like your name, Alexander" and we huff and puff as we write "Alexander" on the blackboard. Immediately one or two children call out, "It must be wheelbarrow." "Why not *cart*?" we ask. "Too *short*!" expostulate several children in unison. So we write "cart" and "wheelbarrow" on the blackboard and everybody gets the point. I hear a muted comment from one child to another, "Look, you can see the *wheel* part and the *barrow* part too."

"But the goat's asleep in the wheelbarrow.

Where shall -- --- --- ----?"
(Picture of goat on wooden fence.)

"Put the goat on top of the g----- g---.

The goat can sleep there very ----

till the --- ----- ---- -- --- -------."

When we get to "garden gate" we put the vital initial letter cues on the blackboard, and a strong response comes through from two or three children, followed by a hum of general approbation. (Sometimes we make the first connection through children's names at the point when that letter-sound association is called for. Most of our phonics is taught in this functional, non-structured way.)

*"But the rooster is roosting on the garden gate.*

*----- ----- - --- --- -------?"*

Now we show the next picture because it is crucial to the context. It's a rooster stuck in a barrel-like tub with a stirring handle alongside. Instead of writing up the initial letters this time, we articulate them — yes, isolate them, "buh ... ch ..." The phonemes have not been isolated in the damaging way of having no possible content, context, significance or brain-triggering function. They have been fed at the exactly appropriate second into brains filled with expectant information.

*"Put the rooster in the b----- ch---,*

*so tight that he can't tw--- or t---*

*till --- --- ----- ---- -- --- -------."*

The children puzzle for a while over the "butter churn," but as soon as some bright spark gets it, the rest of the class perceive the process immediately and concur. This is what I call the communal "Yes, of course!" response. One of the great advantages of communal, participant teaching over competitive, take-your-turn-to-face-the-music teaching is that every learner can be intellectually active with good feeling for most of the time. Another advantage displayed by this particular lesson, is that we can use satisfyingly rich material, too difficult for reading at sight and alone by any child in the group, and yet the slowest participate, cope, and learn.

We have made photo-copies and then transparencies of the next two pages to take advantage of another powerful technique to involve a large group in concurrent problem-solving, progressive exposure. We now use the overhead projector with the text covered by two sheets of paper, one standing below the line to be read and one obscuring that line, which will be exposed progressively by sliding the top sheet sideways. When we turn on the projector light, we are able to see the text on the face of the projector through the paper but it is not projected until we slide the cover sheet. We can stop at any point in a sentence or a word to arouse prediction or discuss and then uncover confirming detail.

> *"But my nice fresh butter is in the churn.*
>
> *Where shall - --- --- ------?"*
>
> *"Put the butter on a string in the garden pool,*
>
> *and it will keep there fr--- and c---*
>
> *till --- ----- ---- -- --- -------."*

As we expose the "p" of "pool" there is some discussion over the merits of "pond" and "pool". We slide the cover sheet backwards, i.e., to the left, and expose the "l". Everyone responds "pool". Rather similarly, when we expose the "fr" of "fresh" some children move straight to the "fresh and cool" based on the rhyme. We discuss what graphic detail we would need to be sure, to *confirm* the hypothesis. We use a pointed pencil or pen to locate particular letters and ask, "What letter would you expect to see here?" This not only makes it possible to teach confirmation or checking directly and with precision but also to develop phonic insights which move from sounds analyzed in spoken words to letters expected on the page. This is an intrinsically easier and more useful way of using the association than by asking children to move from letters to sound associations and then by blending to reach the word. Furthermore, associating from sound to letter is essential to the speller, and it is important to use techniques which actually induce this sound-in-the-word to letter-visualized-in-the-brain type of phonics.

Whenever we are talking about letters we use the letter names rather than the most dominant sound association for that letter. In this way we encourage children to visualize or image print in facilitating both reading and spelling. This also makes it possible for us to talk to children intelligibly about the phonic *options* for a letter or group of letters. The "p" and the "h" in "photo" or "elephant" stand for the sound "f" which is normally written with an "ef".

Sometimes we present *part* of the story through written

cloze, but the nature of the cloze is distinctly different from normal cloze tests in which deletions are made every five or six words, are made regularly without regard to difficulty, function, or teaching objective, do not include an idea of word length or any graphic detail, and require the actual word from the text in order to be marked correct. In putting cloze to instructional use we vary and control all of these factors. In particular we keep to a deletion rate above one in ten words unless structural or syntactic or idiomatic expectations involve whole clusters of words:

> *"Put the figs in the barn on a pile of wh---.*
>
> *They'll keep quite f--- and fr--- and sweet*
>
> *till _____."*
>
> *"But the pig is sleeping on the pile of wheat*
>
> *What shall I -- ---- --- ---?"*
>
> *"Put the pig on a pillow in the feather b--*
>
> *to sn--- and sn---," the old man said,*
>
> *"till _____."*
>
> *"No," said the woman. "I sl--- on the bed.*
>
> *Where shall I lay my funny old h---?"*
>
> *The old man cried, "Put the p-- in the bed!*
>
> *And you can stand on your f---- --- ----*
>
> *till _____."*

At some point we may pause for a moment to let the children think and talk about what is happening in their heads — to develop *their own* metalinguistic explanations and clarifications. We may ask a leading question or two depending on the nature of the cloze activity: "What makes you think it will be such and such?" "How sure can we be that this is such and such?" What more do we need to know to be sure of this word?" "If this word is such and such, what letter would we expect to see here?"

Over the weeks the children's responses to these opportunities for reflection, discovery and clarification become more and more sophisticated. They always bring to the surface the compelling necessity for sense and meaning. They concede the usefulness of predictable structures of rhyme and rhythm. They expose the power of patterns larger than the sentence in determining what a particular word is likely to be. In the end they see that there is not one sacrosanct way of solving problems. Like evidence, each type of cue piles up towards certainty, and they check up on each other and compensate for each other. Sometimes they even contradict each other and in this case it is the weight of evidence that counts, with sense and meaning being the final arbitrators.

At the end of the story, as we all glow in the hilarious beauty of it, we know that many children will return to it many times. Part of the pleasure of the story was the successful cognitive engagement with the text. Solving problems is among the greatest of human pleasures, especially when the problems are relevant and solvable. The whole endeavour of making sense out of written language, even its most strange conventions, can be deeply satisfying and absorbing for children.

The slower children felt a part of the reading and writing community. They were dignified by the experience and not threatened by it. As they return to the story, they will succeed for a number of reasons: the story has high impact and will draw them back like a magnet, the first experience was successful because of the supportive procedures, and while it is still recent all the echoes and the clarifications of that experience will tend towards success in a more independent approach to the text, the structure is highly predictable in many different ways making words like "fresh" and "snooze" pop out with delightful human ease.

Finally, aspects of story pattern and new linguistic structures have been introduced in memorable and generative ways. Several children are likely to attempt a story of their own following this sort of structure. As they come to other stories displaying a similar structure and attempt to read them, perhaps independently, something will go click and a whole train of facilitating expectations will be accessible. More significantly and lastingly, the story will have contributed something important to each child's understanding of the world. Light and all as it is on the surface, and never coming near to stating a moral, it adds something to a child's understanding of human motive and strategy — the story is a little warning about games people play.

*Independent Activity and Related Arts:* After the story the children move off to diverse activity centred on literacy. They are confident and at ease but ready to get their teeth into something. Reading and book-making dominate today, but on other days it may be drama or painting which attract most activity. Operating in twos and threes some of the children socialize in their reading, while some gather round the easel to play at being teacher and class. A few of the children, stimulated by the simple, bold humor of the illustrations explore the style — which had been discussed briefly during the story. They begin with a bold black outline which they later block in with color. Most of these paintings will not be completed for a day or two as children rework and enrich the texture with pastel or collage.

Other children prefer a quiet and private exploration choosing to read old favorites or from the copious supply of simple materials made available for independent reading but seldom taking much instructional time. Some of these have been chosen from the best of materials which would previously have been used as sequential instructional readers. The feeling, "I can read a book all by myself" is evident. Often a child will complete one of these books with great satisfaction in five minutes — about the amount of attention the book deserved. In a structured program the same child may have found himself "on" that book and its exercises and activities for several weeks.

To satisfy the need for a quiet and somewhat private place for reading we have built a "Reading Cave". This is a whale-shaped structure built first with wire netting and then covered by many layers of papier-mâché decorated with donated cans of paint children have brought from home. The cave has an entrance like an igloo and backs onto a window for illumination. With its old cushions and bean bags it is a comfortable and secure retreat.

As the activity time begins we work first with a group who seek our assistance in beginning a "Fire! Fire!" book. The half dozen children suggest some words that rhyme with their names, first or surname. Some work out easily: " 'Give the fireman a call!' said Brett and Paul," and " 'Run as fast as can be!' said Jodie Lee." We didn't think there was a rhyme for "Alexander" until someone came up with "verandah". We gave a little help here since rhyming is not the easiest form of expression for young children, and we came up with, " 'I'm so embarrassed!' said Joanne Harris." The big words, not on any list until middle grades delighted the children and kept popping up in their own writing for weeks after the book came to "publication" as a class venture. The initiating group went off happily to begin the illustrations which gave the final book much of its charm.

Two or three of the least confident children bring familiar books which they wish to share. They are quietly proud of the fact that they *can* read although they are aware that they haven't the fuller competencies of many of the others. We take the opportunity to set up the tape recorder in the comparative quietness of the Cave. We have been supplied on request with a blank tape for each child, and when the opportunity arises naturally we record a short, dated example of volunteered reading. Later we will include some simple reading at sight and use this record to analyze reading progress and needs on an individual basis. We use a modified form of miscue analysis, but there are a number of simple techniques available (Weaver, 1980; Clay, 1980).

One of the good things about the tape recordings is that we don't intervene unless requested by the reader. Now that we have become interested in really listening to children, it is amazing how easy it is to determine how each child is operating, and to be genuinely appreciative of approximation. This concrete form of longitudinal monitoring also proves useful and often a source of delight to parents and to the children themselves nearing the end of the year.

The listening-post is in active use during this time. Sets of materials for group read-along are always available and our library is growing. The children set up and operate the recorder themselves and cooperate in preparing some of the book and author displays we use to brighten up the area. We have begun to prepare some tapes using oral cloze on a relaxed deletion rate of about one in fifteen words. These tapes have been surprisingly popular and it is satisfying to hear the children popping out with the words every ten seconds or so.

There is a great deal of writing going on normally during the activity time. We don't have a "Writing Corner": we have a Publishing House. Materials are always available for making simple books and help is always on hand. However, since this is a developmental literacy program, no correcting is done except on request — and then by collaboration with the author. Invented spelling is encouraged since those who attempt most learn most about the regularities and peculiarities of our spelling system. A letter has been sent home to parents explaining this policy and the longitudinal file of each child's dated writing over a period of months almost invariably displays rapid progress. We use this file with the children themselves and in regular little interviews each child selects from his or her actual writing words they think they would like to be able to spell.

*Round-up:* At the end of each language block the class comes together to share highlights. Today, the group involved with the "Fire! Fire!" book enthuse the others — everyone wants to be in that book. Some more pages are planned of which the most gratifying was:

> *"The fireman's so handsome!"*
>
> *said Natalie Grantham.*

and the closing twist to the plot:

> *"It's just a burnt pizza!"*
>
> *said little Lisa.*

Each child spent some time during the next few days illustrating his or her page. A week after its completion every child in the class could read the "big book" which we finally "published". A sense of authorship had begun to grow making this the first of a long series of books which were brought through satisfying editing to proud publication through both individual and group processes.

## CONCLUDING REMARKS

These examples from the early grades display the *possibility* of teaching literacy in genuinely developmental ways. The ideas may be used to greater or lesser extent as teachers develop confidence and begin to free themselves from dependence on pre-packaged programs. They may be applied with suitable adjustments throughout the elementary school and with emancipating power in remedial or recovery situations. In the middle grades they give added purpose and precision to the well-tried approaches of Individualized Reading and Uninterrupted Sustained Silent Reading. They are plainly sound and sensible in the light of both research and common sense. Because they arise largely from a study of the natural and the actual, they work and, at a time when education is embarrassed by its expenditures, it should be said that they are strikingly economic of resources when compared with the heavily structured programs of the day.[11]

Of greatest importance in naturalizing early literacy instruction, however, are the professional priorities for both the teachers and their clients. In understanding the nature of reading and writing as developmental tasks, teachers find their rights to decision-making restored and clarified. The techniques now at their disposal, ratified both by research and by what is most sensible in the real world of learning, make it possible for them to control the success level of literacy tasks for all their children each day. They may do this in an environment rich with all we enjoy most in literature without fear that children will fail because of the richness. It may also be an environment uncontaminated by the meaningless, boring, or threatening elements that have too often been written into instructional programs imposed from outside the professional relationship between teachers and clients.[12]

Our principal options in the past have tended to be barren

and factional ones. Certainly the point of view presented here as a reading of language and learning as we face them in the early eighties will not fit into any factional framework such as Traditionalism or Progressivism. Yet it is simple and clear. The information at our disposal today gives a platform or stance strong enough to sustain and direct change in matters critical to our professional development. It is also a stance which accepts the open and scientific and skeptical approach to complex matters, one which leaves us all the room we need for the research and debate essential to any ongoing explanation of human development or education.

# NOTES

---

It is ironic that as research has increasingly stressed the central importance of teachers they have been progressively stripped of their professional functions. Those forces which have downgraded teacher functions are the same forces which have demanded formal accountability and funded the illusion of "teacher-proof" materials. It is rather like bringing in a crudely designed machine to carry out complex tasks for which it was not designed and then holding the operators responsible for resultant defects.

A profession cannot operate without decision-making at the client interface, and accountability must be controlled by natural or judicial processes which arise from experience in the profession. Too many test constructors and psychologists, for instance, do not belong to the profession of teaching — they have no experience in it nor are they oriented towards its functions. Their exploitation of political and administrative prejudices distance them still further from genuine professional concerns which are always and inevitably concerned with client welfare — in the case of education, with pupil welfare.

The demands by administrators for "teacher-proof" materials strikes at the roots of professionalism. How can you improve professional services by rendering your professionals powerless to make decisions which affect their clients? Furthermore, how can you avoid this message of contempt being passed down through the demeaned teachers to the clients themselves? Research is clear that such negative management perverts the true functions of teaching, while at the same time it creates an enormously expensive and self-serving infrastructure ill-adapted to educational purposes.

Research of the seventies and eighties is clear that those extrinsic structures by which the influence of teachers is bypassed — namely methodologies and tightly prescriptive, published programs — are negligible factors in achieving educational ends. The telling relationships are those between confident teachers, participant learners, and worthy materials and ideas judged by the standards of human excellence.

It is far too easy, however, to blame educational publishers for the quality of materials used almost universally in the schools while at the same time excluding them from the central forums of the profession. We press them to perform miracles or magic — such as produce satisfying books for adolescents at a six year readability level. In the end we purchase from publishers almost exactly what we deserve including the deceits of magic-makers. It is easy to supply lies to those who have seriously asked for them.

### Note 2

The inability of opposing models of reading to account for automaticity and its development during learning, especially the internal contradictions within both the "top-down" and the "bottom-up" models, leads me to favor interactive models which address themselves to this crucial enigma. How do we teach reading (or writing) in such a way as most rapidly and directly to facilitate those astonishingly rapid automatic responses which are so essential to language operation? How does the speaker control lips, tongue and vocal cords without consciously choosing a single phoneme or having the time to? The teaching of phonics as an unremittingly conscious and deliberative process on the one hand, (bottom-up over-stress), and the ponderous cognitive operations which seem to be implied by a consciously manipulated hypothesis/test strategy on the other, both fail to illuminate this process to any degree.

In a clearly reasoned article Stanovich (1980) seems to go furthest in accounting for the available data in this area. By giving prominence to the part which compensatory processes may play in the acquisition of reading, his model offers some rational avenues to account for automaticity. Perhaps in the application of an already automated system to early reading — operating from the known, familiar and habituated to the unknown and problematic — successful learners are able to maintain that necessary level of automaticity and fluency required by the brain in coordinating complex behaviors at a rate much faster than conscious deliberation would allow.

It is my own tentative belief that successful learners require "automating strategies" in order to make optimum progress. Such strategies, observable in the natural behavior of precocious learners, as the re-processing of favorite text in print-attending situations, responding to pleasingly repetitive text such as cumulative or cyclic stories, read-along participation in many text-tied settings, and a variety of cloze, or participation-inducing procedures, all provide this essential bridge to natural automaticity. Once the problem is recognized as being central it should not be difficult to research.

### Note 3

The way in which we separate word perception from comprehension may account for our worst failures in teaching literacy. It is a classically adult and academic abuse of logic — never seen in real life except under extreme duress. Watching an infant struggling successfully with learning to speak we note a constant wrestling with detail in an attempt to achieve purpose and meaning. At no time do we ever see an infant working in a curriculum which separates item from function, part from whole. We do, indeed, observe infants practising parts or leapfrogging parts to approximations of the whole, but both processes occur as linguistically functional objectives.

It would seem that, even in trying to articulate, it is necessary to keep the target detail blanketed or supported by the total functional target or whole meaning. The wholistic blanketing facilitates item learning or mastery. We could also hypothesize for the more covert processes of learning to listen — the oral correlative of learning to read — that the encapsulation of a new or confusing item within both a linguistic whole and its real function may be even more crucial to learning. Using the strategy of reproducing the whole in order to master the parts recommends itself even from a crudely stimulus-response point of view, in that the recall of the whole recreates in memory the appropriate model in which the target item was presented and with which the response must be compared.

The playful syntactic and structural repetitions and transformations of infants in learning speech ("Me love Mummy!", "Me love Daddy!", "Me love dolly!", "Mummy love Daddy!", "Mummy love Rebecca!") are mirrored in the old favorite stories and poems, and they facilitate reading in a similar way.

> *I have run away from an old man,*
>
> *And an old woman,*
>
> *And a boy,*
>
> *And some farmers, etc.*

Infants become preoccupied with mastering linguistic items only in so far as those items occur in currently meaningful linguistic and real situations. (The mastery of "telfishon" is worth practising if it can be intelligibly produced in a sweetly upraised intonation following "wash", as is currently occurring in the learning of our two and a half year old.) I have found no exceptions to this rule in a long life of forced and unforced infant watching. Strange that we literacy teachers should so forcibly, and with almost religious fanaticism over the years, abuse such a universally apparent principle of language learning. Let's return to the common sense of teaching item detail within linguistically functioning situations. See also Note 1 re automaticity in language learning.

## Note 4

The principles and tendencies we have discussed in this chapter have not been applied very generally or systematically to the remedial setting. The medical model of test, diagnosis and treatment has sadly obscured a problem which is primarily educational and linguistic. A confusing new culture centred on "learning disabilities" may have explanatory power but it lacks clear and helpful guidelines for educational action. It trades natural learning procedures for extravagances of manipulation such as "mastery learning", the human priorities of clienthood for labels and isolating procedures,' and sensible, research-based understanding of learning confusions for tenuously based and compellingly fatalistic etiological explanations.

Some practical suggestions will be found in Smith (1973), Holdaway (1979 & 1980), Weaver (1980), Hittleman (1978), and Aulls (1982). The suggestions in Holdaway are largely based on clinical experience.

*Note 5*

Working from a rich flow of literature through the program it is a simple matter to develop relevant vocabulary and syntactical activities from favorite, familiar material. If for instance we have recently enjoyed Ezra Keats, *Apartment 3*, and Joan Heilbroner's, *This is the House Where Jack Lived*, (or other housy books), we may explore the vocabulary of living places, and perhaps suggest that some children may like to write their own versions of the old "House That Jack Built" tale substituting "hotel", or "penthouse" or "tent" with appropriate adjustments.

This is an ideal time for a very brief exercise in what the linguists call "substitution tables." However, instead of using the deadly dull language so often associated with structural drills in second language teaching, we begin from some high impact, familiar sentence from the literature such as, "Whose that tripping/running/jumping/scampering/dancing/etc. over my bridge?" Favorite sentences may be cut up for resorting and sequencing, and so on. Many fine examples of sentence manipulation will be found in the Teachers' Manuals to the Bill Martin & Peggy Brogan, *Sounds of Language* series, published by Holt, Rinehart and Winston.

*Note 6*

This book and a number of others of the *Instant Readers* have been produced in kit format by Holt, Rinehart and Winston Ltd., Toronto.

*Note 7*

The notion of "word" is so fundamental to us as adults that we feel it is sort of self-evident, and we find it difficult to understand that many youngsters enter school without a clear notion of a "word" even for oral language. They now face the task of applying the fuzzy tag to a set of written symbols demarcated by spaces on left and right. Confusion at this deep conceptual level is more likely to cause problems in early reading and writing than most of the trivial items contained in "readiness programs."

Careful pointing in familiar, enlarged text seems to clarify this confusion most rapidly and naturally. The use of a variety of masking devices in enlarged text helps to direct attention and provide impact.

*Note 8*

The points made in Note 7 above are very relevant here. Directing visual attention to details in clear, enlarged and *familiar* text provides a bridge from oral to written symbols without the possibility of confusion. Children are able to observe visual correlatives for *orally secure items* in this way.

Regular exposure to isolated letters and words, such as on flashcards, can be expected only to confound an initial confusion and raise anxiety to levels which exclude positive learning. See also Note 3 above.

*Note 9*

A growing body of ethnographic research, represented here by Nathan *et al.* (1982), emphasizes the vital role played by early exploration of writing in opening up the concepts of reading and written language. It would appear that for many children the development of writing insights and skills precedes the development of reading. We seem to have been quite mistaken in making the adult assumption that reading precedes, or should precede, learning about writing.

*Note 10*

A high quality miscue is one which retains syntactical function and does not alter the basic meaning of the text — it is a miscue displaying appropriate priorities. A low quality of miscue is one which breaches syntactic and/or semantic appropriateness, and often takes the form of a verbal item or non-word suggested by aspects of grapho-phonics alone. All miscues stem from *some* rational impulse — from some more or less adequate strategy. Bearing in mind the proper uses of approximation, we should attempt to determine for each miscue the rational grounds, incomplete or mistaken, upon which the reader's response was based. This provides a basis for discussion which will be positive, intelligible and helpful to the reader. See Weaver (1980) for a simple and useful rationale.

*Note 11*

There are several reasons for this economy. Despite the fact that dozens of books from the open literature will be used in a natural, developmental literacy program, the following points indicate how this massive increase in quantity of material processed may yet be less costly in dollar terms:
   (i) Books are used and purchased in single copy or a few small group sets. Every child does not require a copy.
  (ii) Most schools already have access to a wide selection of underused literature.
 (iii) Many trade books, especially those in paperback, are much cheaper than basals.
 (iv) Each favorite book is likely to be used extensively by many children for many purposes. Children seldom wish to use their basals in this intensive way and often it would be inappropriate for them to do so.
  (v) The major expenses of basals arise from the cost of ancillary material —
      a. Expensive manuals,
      b. Expendable workbooks,
      c. Ditto sheets and
      d. Tests.
These items have little place in a fully functioning developmental program although the basal readers themselves have many valuable uses.

*Note 12*

When a teacher is using a structured, basal program, whether out of conviction, insecurity, or through school policy, a number of unwritten, unsubstantiated and sometimes quite false assumptions tend to operate:

(i) The series was written by "experts" and their judgements are superior to mine.

(In fact, a reliable professional judgement must always be an on-the-spot, knowledge-of-client judgement. The function of experts is to help us understand and interpret our data, not to make decisions for us.)

(ii) The sequence of skills and sub-skills has been scientifically ratified and I should not depart from it to any significant extent for any child.

(There is no scientifically ratified sequence of skills in reading development. Every series uses a different sequence and this is determined by opinion rather than science. A truly developmental sequence is one displayed in the behavior and characteristics of the pupil. When basal sequence charts are presented as "developmental", this is a misuse of the term.)

(iii) If I leave out any phases of the system, I feel guilty.

(No professional guidance material should induce guilt. The only thing more destructive of teaching than guilt feelings is attempting to teach blindly what is not personally understood.)

(iv) Task success of all children can be controlled by the devices and progressions built into the materials by those who are experts in readability.

(In fact, the whole concept of readability as we have understood it in the last thirty years is being discredited by research of several kinds. No formula for readability can approach accuracy without taking into account the other agent in the transaction, the reader. Readability may also be controlled by powerful strategies of teaching and learning as we saw in Chapter 2. These strategies go far beyond "readability" measures in controlling task difficulty with precision.)

(v) Because the basal program provides all the essentials, there is less work for the teacher.

(The "work" of a teacher, like that of any professional, must be measured in terms of the amount of time, energy, and personal stress required to achieve a given educational end. Certainly, the structured basal program demands less time and effort of the teacher, but since it fails so often to achieve desirable educational ends, the saving is illusory, and the personal stress is likely to escalate.)

# REFERENCES

Aulls, Mark. (1982) *Developing Readers in Today's Elementary Schools.* Toronto: Allyn and Bacon.

Barbe, Walter B., and Abbott, Jerry L. (1975) *Personalized Reading Instruction.* West Nyack, N.Y.: Parker.

Barrett, F.L. (1982) *A Teacher's Guide to Shared Reading.* Toronto: Scholastic.

Bettelheim, Bruno, and Zelan, Karen. (1982) *On Learning to Read: The Child's Fascination with Meaning.* New York: Knopf.

Bissex, Glenda. (1982) *GNYS AT WRK: A Child Learns to Write and Read.* Cambridge, Mass.: Cambridge University Press.

Bormuth, John R. (1978) "Literacy Policy and Reading and Writing Instruction," in *Perspectives on Literacy,* eds. R. Beach and P.D. Pearson, pp. 13-41. College of Education, University of Minnesota.

Britton, James. (1970) *Language and Learning.* Harmondsworth: Penguin.

Butler, Dorothy. (1979) *Cushla and Her Books.* Auckland: Hodder and Stoughton.

Chomsky, Carol. (1976) "After Decoding: What?" *Language Arts,* Vol. 53, No. 3, pp. 288-296, 314.

Clay, Marie. (1967) "The Reading Behavior of Five Year Old Children: A Research Report." *New Zealand Journal of Educational Studies,* Vol. 12, No. 1, pp. 11-31.

Clay, Marie. (1980) *Reading: The Patterning of Complex Behavior.* 2nd Edition. Auckland: Heinemann.

Ellis, M.J. (1973) *Why People Play.* New Jersey: Prentice-Hall.

Gamble, Trevor J., and McFetridge, Patricia A. (1981) "Children, Similes,

Metaphors, and Reading Go Together." *Reading-Canada-Lecture*, Vol. 1, No. 1, pp. 29-35.

Goodman, K.S. (1965) "A Linguistic Study of Cues and Miscues in Reading." *Elementary English*, 42, pp. 639-643.

Goodman, Y.M., and Burke, C.L. (1972) *Reading Miscue Inventory*. New York: Macmillan.

Goodman, Y.M., and Burke, C.L. (1980) *Reading Strategies: Focus on Comprehension*. New York: Holt, Rinehart and Winston.

Gough, Philip B. (1976) "One Second of Reading," in *Theoretical Models and Processes of Reading*, 2nd edition, eds. H. Singer and R.B. Ruddell, pp. 509-535. Newark, Del.: International Reading Association.

Graves, Donald H. (1983) *Writing: Teachers and Children at Work*. Exeter, N.H.: Heinemann.

Guthrie, John T. (1981) "Reading in New Zealand: Achievement and Volume." *Reading Research Quarterly*, Vol. 17, No. 1, pp. 6-27.

Hittleman, Daniel. (1978) *Developmental Reading: A Psycholinguistic Perspective*. Chicago: Rand McNally.

Holdaway, Don. (1979) *The Foundations of Literacy*. Sydney: Scholastic.

Holdaway, Don. (1980) *Independence in Reading*. 2nd Edition. Sydney: Scholastic.

Hoskisson, Kenneth. (1975) "The Many Facets of Assisted Reading." *Elementary English*, Vol. 52, No. 3, pp. 312-315.

Huey, E.B. (1908) *The Psychology and Pedagogy of Reading*. Cambridge, Mass.: M.I.T. Press.

Lefevre, Carl A. (1964) *Linguistics and the Teaching of Reading*. New York: McGraw Hill.

McCracken, Marlene and Robert. (1979) *Reading, Writing and Language: A Practical Guide to Primary Teachers*. Winnipeg: Peguis.

Martin, Bill, and Brogan, Peggy. (1972) Teacher's Guide to *Sounds of Language* series. New York: Holt, Rinehart and Winston.

Mason, Jana M. (1980) "When Do Children Begin to Read: An Exploration of Four Year Old Children's Letter and Word Reading Competence." *Reading Research Quarterly*, Vol. 15, No. 2, pp. 203-227.

Read, Charles. (1982) "Writing is Not the Inverse of Reading for Young Children," in *Writing: The Natural Development and Teaching of Written Communication*, eds. Frederickson, Whiteman, and Dominic. Hillsdale, N.J.: Erlbaum Assoc.

Robinson, Susan. (1973) "Predicting Early Reading Progress." Unpublished thesis, University of Auckland.

Smith, Frank. (1973) "Twelve Easy Ways to Make Learning to Read Difficult," in *Psycholinguistics and Reading*, ed. Frank Smith, pp. 183-196. New York: Holt, Rinehart and Winston.

Smith, Frank. (1975) *Comprehension and Learning*. New York: Holt, Rinehart and Winston.

Smith, Frank. (1978) *Understanding Reading*. 2nd Edition. New York: Holt, Rinehart and Winston.

Smith, Frank. (1982) *Writing and the Writer*. New York: Holt, Rinehart and Winston.

Stanovich, Keith E. (1980) "Toward an Interactive-compensatory Model of Individual Differences in the Development of Reading Fluency." *Reading Research Quarterly*, Vol. 16, No. 1, pp. 32-71.

Teale, William H. (1981) "Parents Reading to Their Children: What We Know and What We Need to Know." *Language Arts*, Vol. 58, No. 8, pp. 902-912.

Temple, Charles A., Nathan, Ruth G., and Burris, Nancy A. (1982) *The Beginnings of Writing*. Boston: Allyn and Bacon.

Terry, Pamela R. (1976) "The Effect of Orthographic Transformations Upon Speed and Accuracy of Semantic Categorizations." (Abstracted Report) *Reading Research Quarterly*, Vol. 12, No. 2, pp. 166-175.

Veatch, Jeanette. (1968) *How to Teach Reading with Children's Books*. New York: Citation Press.

Weaver, Constance. (1980) *Psycholinguistics and Reading: From Process to Practice*. Cambridge: Winthrop.

## Other titles of interest:

**GIVING TEACHING BACK TO TEACHERS: A CRITICAL INTRODUCTION TO CURRICULUM THEORY**
Robin Barrow

**THE COUNTRY OF THE YOUNG: UNITS IN CANADIAN LITERATURE FOR ELEMENTARY AND SECONDARY SCHOOLS**
Don Gutteridge

**BRAVE SEASON: READING AND THE LANGUAGE ARTS IN GRADES SEVEN TO TEN**
Don Gutteridge

**STARTING THE ARK IN THE DARK: TEACHING CANADIAN LITERATURE IN HIGH SCHOOL**
Ian Underhill

**LABYRINTHS OF LITERACY: REFLECTIONS ON LITERACY PAST AND PRESENT**
Harvey Graff

**TEACHING AS STORY TELLING: AN ALTERNATIVE APPROACH TO TEACHING & CURRICULUM IN THE ELEMENTARY SCHOOL**
Kieran Egan

**INCREDIBLE JOURNEYS, NEW APPROACHES TO THE NOVEL IN GRADES 7 - 10, A HANDBOOK FOR TEACHERS**
Don Gutteridge

Further details from:
**THE ALTHOUSE PRESS**
Faculty of Education
The University of Western Ontario
1137 Western Road
LONDON, Ontario, Canada
N6G 1G7
Tel: (519) 661-2096